HAL•LEONARD
INSTRUMENTAL
PLAY-ALONG

TENOR SAX

Andrew Lloyd Webber
Classics

How To Use The CD Accompaniment:
A melody cue appears on the right channel only. If your CD player has a balance adjustment, you can adjust the volume of the melody by turning down the right channel.

Andrew Lloyd Webber® is a trademark owned by Andrew Lloyd Webber
Technicolor® is the registered trademark of the Technicolor group of companies.

Performance Warning:
Public Performances of this work may only be given in premises licensed by ASCAP (The American Society Of Composers, Authors and Publishers).
Please note that such performances must on no account use any form of costume, staging, character representation, choreography, props or dramatic lighting effects. All dramatic stage rights and the right to perform the work in anything other than a normal concert format are strictly prohibited.

ISBN 0-634-06156-9

HAL•LEONARD®
CORPORATION
7777 W. BLUEMOUND RD. P.O. BOX 13819 MILWAUKEE, WI 53213

Visit Hal Leonard Online at
www.halleonard.com

THE PHANTOM OF THE OPERA
from THE PHANTOM OF THE OPERA

Music by ANDREW LLOYD WEBBER
Lyrics by CHARLES HART
Additional Lyrics by RICHARD STILGOE and MIKE BATT

CD
◆**1**: With melody cue
◆**2**: Accompaniment only

TENOR SAX

Moderately

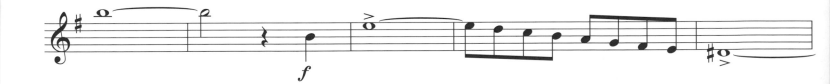

DON'T CRY FOR ME ARGENTINA
from EVITA

CD
3: With melody cue
4: Accompaniment only

Words by TIM RICE
Music by ANDREW LLOYD WEBBER

TENOR SAX

CLOSE EVERY DOOR
from JOSEPH AND THE AMAZING TECHNICOLOR® DREAMCOAT

Music by ANDREW LLOYD WEBBER
Lyrics by TIM RICE

CD

5 : With melody cue
6 : Accompaniment only

TENOR SAX

Small notes optional

molto rit.

AS IF WE NEVER SAID GOODBYE
from SUNSET BOULEVARD

Music by ANDREW LLOYD WEBBER
Lyrics by DON BLACK and CHRISTOPHER HAMPTON,
with contributions by AMY POWERS

CD

7 : With melody cue

8 : Accompaniment only

TENOR SAX

EVERYTHING'S ALRIGHT
from JESUS CHRIST SUPERSTAR

Words by TIM RICE
Music by ANDREW LLOYD WEBBER

CD
◆ **9** : With melody cue
◆ **10** : Accompaniment only

TENOR SAX

GUS: THE THEATRE CAT
from CATS

Music by ANDREW LLOYD WEBBER
Text by T.S. ELIOT

CD

◆11: With melody cue

◆12: Accompaniment only

TENOR SAX

9

UNEXPECTED SONG
from SONG & DANCE

Music by ANDREW LLOYD WEBBER
Lyrics by DON BLACK

CD

🔺13 : With melody cue

🔺14 : Accompaniment only

TENOR SAX

THE MUSIC OF THE NIGHT
from THE PHANTOM OF THE OPERA

Music by ANDREW LLOYD WEBBER
Lyrics by CHARLES HART
Additional Lyrics by RICHARD STILGOE

CD

15: With melody cue
16: Accompaniment only

TENOR SAX

LOVE CHANGES EVERYTHING
from ASPECTS OF LOVE

Music by ANDREW LLOYD WEBBER
Lyrics by DON BLACK and CHARLES HART

CD
17 : With melody cue
18 : Accompaniment only

TENOR SAX

WHISTLE DOWN THE WIND
from WHISTLE DOWN THE WIND

Music by ANDREW LLOYD WEBBER
Lyrics by JIM STEINMAN

CD

◆**19** : With melody cue
◆**20** : Accompaniment only

TENOR SAX

OUR KIND OF LOVE
from THE BEAUTIFUL GAME

Music by ANDREW LLOYD WEBBER
Lyrics by BEN ELTON

TENOR SAX

GO GO GO JOSEPH
from JOSEPH AND THE AMAZING TECHNICOLOR® DREAMCOAT

Music by ANDREW LLOYD WEBBER
Lyrics by TIM RICE

CD
23: With melody cue
24: Accompaniment only

TENOR SAX

PLAY MORE OF YOUR FAVORITE SONGS

WITH GREAT INSTRUMENTAL PLAY ALONG PACKS FROM HAL LEONARD

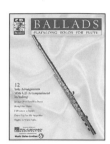

Ballads
Solo arrangements of 12 songs: Bridge Over Troubled Water • Bring Him Home • Candle in the Wind • Don't Cry for Me Argentina • I Don't Know How to Love Him • Imagine • Killing Me Softly with His Song • Nights in White Satin • Wonderful Tonight • more.

00841445 Flute.............$10.95
00841446 Clarinet $10.95
00841447 Alto Sax...........................$10.95
00841448 Tenor Sax........................$10.95
00841449 Trumpet $10.95
00841450 Trombone $10.95
00841451 Violin $10.95

Band Jam
12 band favorites complete with accompaniment CD, including: Born to Be Wild • Get Ready for This • I Got You (I Feel Good) • Rock & Roll – Part II (The Hey Song) • Twist and Shout • We Will Rock You • Wild Thing • Y.M.C.A • and more.

00841232 Flute.............$10.95
00841233 Clarinet $10.95
00841234 Alto Sax...........................$10.95
00841235 Trumpet $10.95
00841236 Horn $10.95
00841237 Trombone $10.95
00841238 Violin $10.95

Disney Movie Hits
Now solo instrumentalists can play along with a dozen favorite songs from Disney blockbusters, including: Beauty and the Beast • Circle of Life • Cruella De Vil • Go the Distance • God Help the Outcasts • Kiss the Girl • When She Loved Me • A Whole New World • and more.

00841420 Flute........................$12.95
00841421 Clarinet $12.95
00841422 Alto Sax...........................$12.95
00841423 Trumpet $12.95
00841424 French Horn $12.95
00841425 Trombone/Baritone...........$12.95
00841686 Tenor Sax........................$12.95
00841687 Oboe...............................$12.95
00841688 Mallet Percussion $12.95
00841426 Violin $12.95
00841427 Viola $12.95
00841428 Cello $12.95

FOR MORE INFORMATION, SEE YOUR LOCAL MUSIC DEALER, OR WRITE TO:

HAL•LEONARD™
CORPORATION
7777 W. BLUEMOUND RD. P.O. BOX 13819 MILWAUKEE, WI 53213

Visit Hal Leonard online at **www.halleonard.com**

Disney Solos
An exciting collection of 12 solos with full-band accompaniment on CD. Songs include: Be Our Guest • Can You Feel the Love Tonight • Colors of the Wind • Reflection • Under the Sea • You've Got a Friend in Me • Zero to Hero • and more.

00841404 Flute $12.95
00841405 Clarinet/Tenor Sax $12.95
00841406 Alto Sax...........................$12.95
00841407 Horn $12.95
00841408 Trombone $12.95
00841409 Trumpet $12.95
00841410 Violin $12.95
00841411 Viola $12.95
00841412 Cello $12.95
00841506 Oboe...............................$12.95
00841553 Mallet Percussion $12.95

Easy Disney Favorites
13 Disney favorites for solo instruments: Bibbidi-Bobbidi-Boo • It's a Small World • Let's Go Fly a Kite • Mickey Mouse March • A Spoonful of Sugar • Toyland March • Winnie the Pooh • The Work Song • Zip-A-Dee-Doo-Dah • and many more.

00841371 Flute $12.95
00841477 Clarinet $12.95
00841478 Alto Sax...........................$12.95
00841479 Trumpet $12.95
00841480 Trombone $12.95
00841372 Violin $12.95
00841481 Viola $12.95
00841482 Cello/Bass $12.95

Favorite Movie Themes
13 themes, including: *An American Symphony* from Mr. Holland's Opus • Braveheart • Chariots of Fire • Forrest Gump – Main Title • Theme from *Jurassic Park* • Mission: Impossible Theme • and more.

00841166 Flute $10.95
00841167 Clarinet.........$10.95
00841168 Trumpet/Tenor Sax $10.95
00841169 Alto Sax...........................$10.95
00841170 Trombone $10.95
00841171 F Horn $10.95
00841296 Violin $10.95

Jazz & Blues
14 songs: Cry Me a River • Fever • Fly Me to the Moon • God Bless' the Child • Harlem Nocturne • Moonglow • A Night in Tunisia • One Note Samba • Satin Doll • Take the "A" Train • Yardbird Suite • and more.

00841438 Flute $10.95
00841439 Clarinet..........$10.95
00841440 Alto Sax...........................$10.95
00841441 Trumpet $10.95
00841442 Tenor Sax........................$10.95
00841443 Trombone $10.95
00841444 Violin $10.95

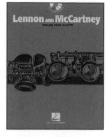

Lennon and McCartney Solos
11 favorites: All My Loving • Can't Buy Me Love • Eleanor Rigby • The Long and Winding Road • Ticket to Ride • Yesterday • and more.

00841542 Flute.............$10.95
00841543 Clarinet $10.95
00841544 Alto Sax........$10.95
00841545 Tenor Sax........................$10.95
00841546 Trumpet $10.95
00841547 Horn $10.95
00841548 Trombone $10.95
00841549 Violin $10.95
00841625 Viola $10.95
00841626 Cello $10.95

Movie & TV Themes
12 favorite themes: A Whole New World • Where Everybody Knows Your Name • Moon River • Theme from Schindler's List • Theme from Star Trek® • You Must Love Me • and more.

00841452 Flute.............$10.95
00841453 Clarinet $10.95
00841454 Alto Sax........$10.95
00841455 Tenor Sax........................$10.95
00841456 Trumpet $10.95
00841457 Trombone $10.95
00841458 Violin $10.95

Sound of Music
9 songs: Climb Ev'ry Mountain • Do-Re-Mi • Edelweiss • The Lonely Goatherd • Maria • My Favorite Things • Sixteen Going on Seventeen • So Long, Farewell • The Sound of Music.

00841582 Flute.............$10.95
00841583 Clarinet $10.95
00841584 Alto Sax..........$10.95
00841585 Tenor Sax........................$10.95
00841586 Trumpet $10.95
00841587 Horn $10.95
00841588 Trombone $10.95
00841589 Violin $10.95
00841590 Viola $10.95
00841591 Cello $10.95

Worship Solos
11 top worship songs: Come, Now Is the Time to Worship • Draw Me Close • Firm Foundation • I Could Sing of Your Love Forever • Open the Eyes of My Heart • Shout to the North • and more.

00841836 Flute...............$12.95
00841837 Oboe...............$12.95
00841838 Clarinet $12.95
00841839 Alto Sax...........................$12.95
00841840 Tenor Sax........................$12.95
00841841 Trumpet $12.95
00841842 Horn $12.95
00841843 Trombone $12.95
00841844 Violin $12.95
00841845 Viola $12.95
00841846 Cello $12.95